The Stories Behind

by Wendy Body

with thanks to **Joanne Ely** for undertaking ~~research~~

Contents

Longman

Edinburgh Gate
Harlow, Essex

Judith Nicholls

Judith Nicholls wrote the story *Ben Biggins' Tummy*. She says that she knows a little boy who looks like Ben Biggins … but he is not as cheeky! She liked the idea of making up stories about a little boy who can be a bit naughty!

Most of the time Judith writes poetry. She writes for children of all ages and she is a very famous **poet**. She has written or put together over 40 books of poetry.

Judith Nicholls

When she is writing, she chooses each word very carefully. She makes sure that it sounds just right. Judith started writing poetry when she was a teenager. She was very shy about talking to people, so sometimes she used to write things down.

"I could work out what I wanted to say and how to say it. No one need ever see or hear it unless I wanted them to!"

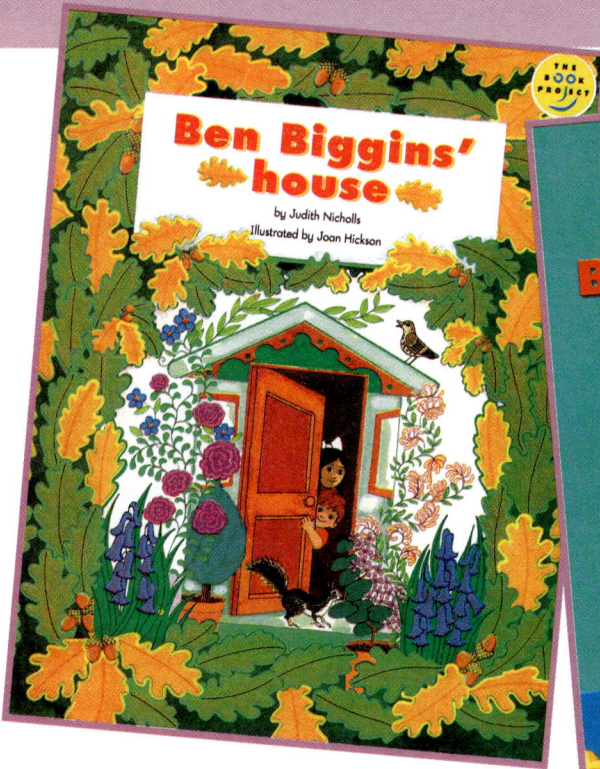

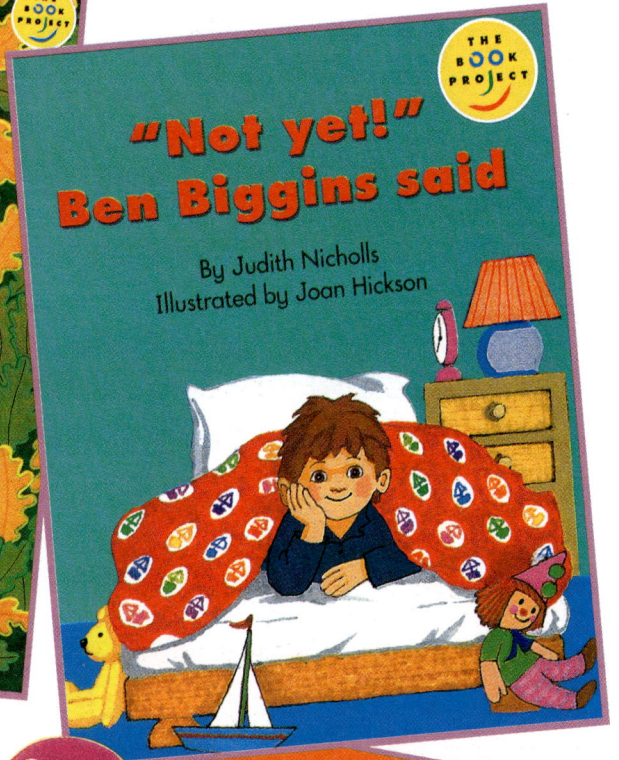

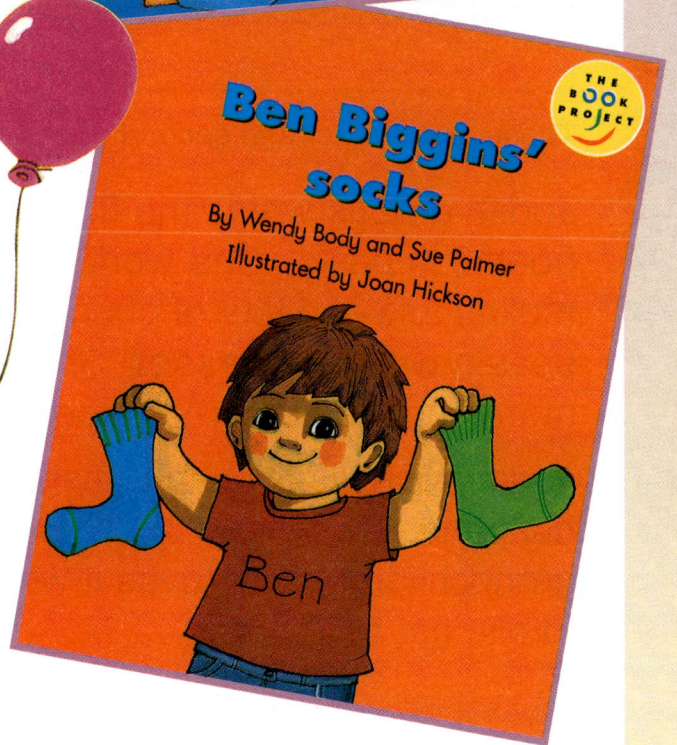

Ben Biggins' house

by Judith Nicholls

Illustrated by Joan Hickson

"Not yet!" Ben Biggins said

By Judith Nicholls

Illustrated by Joan Hickson

Ben Biggins' socks

By Wendy Body and Sue Palmer

Illustrated by Joan Hickson

Ben Biggins

We are? dippers darters

[The] dippers, [the] darters,
[the] dancers through waves
Pipper?
The divers the sliders hiders
sliders
from secret sea-cave?
of deep ocean-Cave

We dip,
dart, etc.
brave?
dare

We curl and we weave
Curl   Swerve
arch

We reach?   we fly
? arch
?
[over] invisible ardros bridges
ocean
Sea to sky

shimmering
ebony
linking   tack?   stitching
air   arching   stitching   ~thread
dare   lace
twist
tur

DOLPHIN DANCE

We are dippers and divers
from secret sea-caves.
We're darters and gliders,
we dance through the waves.

spiral
?   We curve and we curl,
Swerve   we weave as we fly,
            stitching shimmering arches
            from ocean to sky.

Judith Nicholls

rainbow
ebony bridges

circle
bow   arc
arch
band

twist?   spiral & swerve

weave
We arch and we curl,
we curve as we fly,   bridges
stitch shimmering arches
from ocean to sky

We spiral & curl,
we weave as we fly,
stitch'n arches
from ocean to sky

high

curves
+ weaves

These are the first and second drafts of Judith's poem "Dolphin Dance"

Judith always writes the first **drafts** of her poems in pencil. She works on a poem and makes lots and lots of changes. Then she uses a **word processor**. She will often make more changes before the poem is finished.

Judith Nicholls lives in Wiltshire with her husband. They have three children and four grandchildren. She loves it when all the family get together!

Her children had lots of pets when they were small. They had a dog, a cat, a chicken, gerbils, rabbits, guinea pigs, budgies and goldfish!

Judith likes going sailing with her husband. She also plays the piano and likes reading, cooking and walking. But one of the things that Judith likes best is writing.

She says, "I think everyone likes to make something – a cake, a model, a dress, a painting, a chair. I like to make something with words."

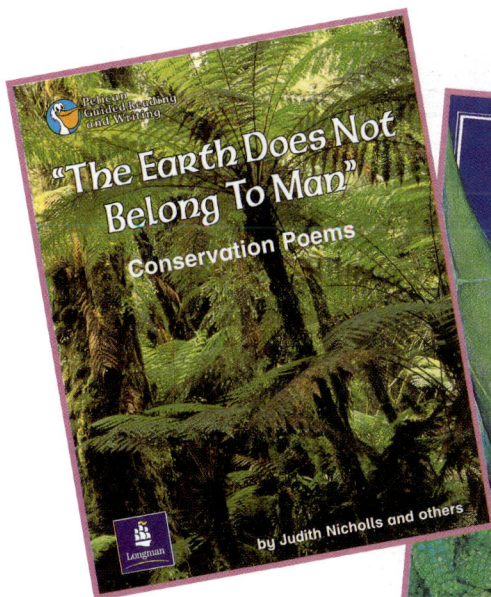

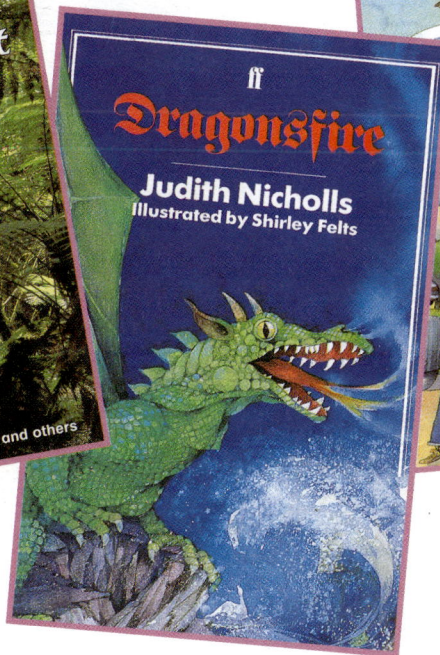

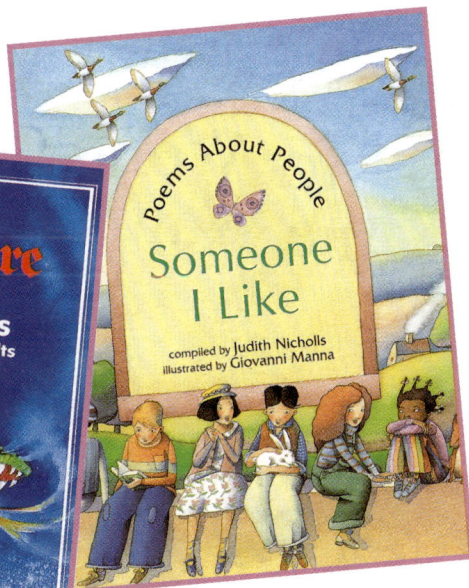

Allan Ahlberg

Allan Ahlberg wrote *Mrs Plug the Plumber*. This is one of the "Happy Families" books. Have you read any of them?

When Allan left school, he worked as a grave-digger. Then he trained to become a teacher. Allan was a teacher for ten years before he became a **full-time writer**.

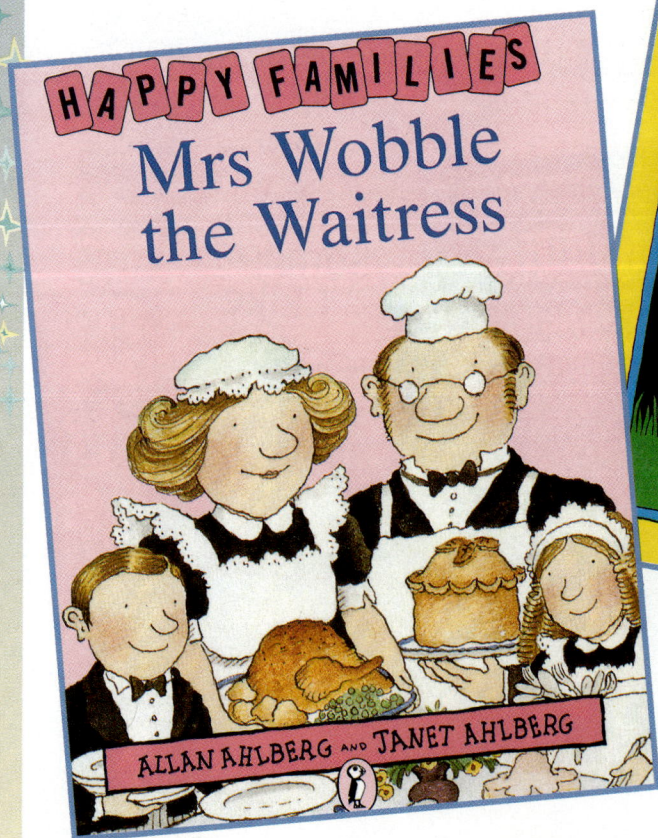

HAPPY FAMILIES
Mrs Wobble the Waitress
ALLAN AHLBERG AND JANET AHLBERG

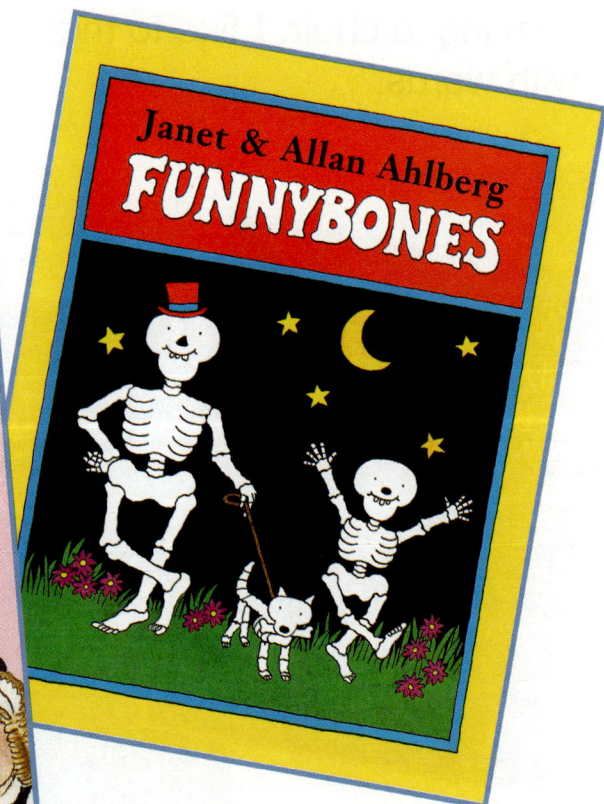

Janet & Allan Ahlberg
FUNNYBONES

He has been writing children's books for about 25 years. Most of them are very funny – like the "Funnybones" stories. Does he only write books for children?

He says, "When I get up in the morning and sit down to write, it is some kind of children's book that comes out."

Allan Ahlberg

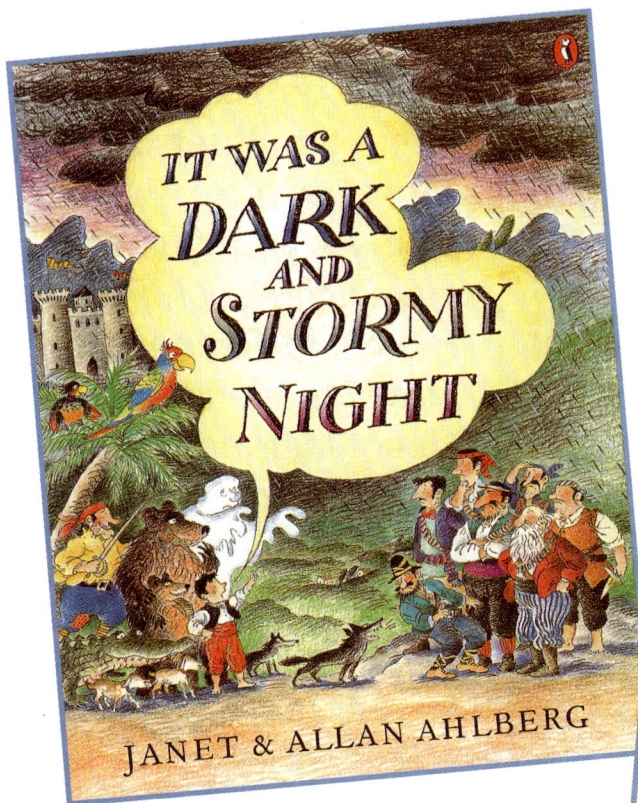

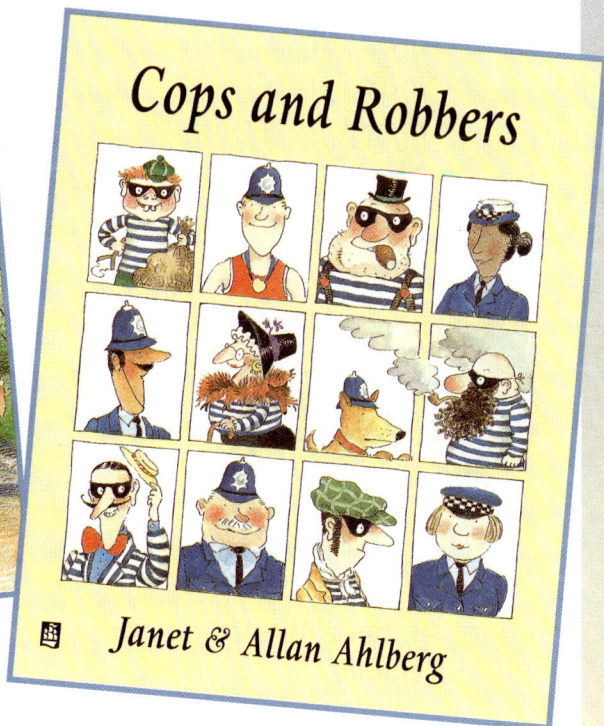

JANET & ALLAN AHLBERG

Cops and Robbers

Janet & Allan Ahlberg

Allan was adopted when he was a baby. His life was not always easy. His family did not have very much money. When he was a boy, he moved four times in six years.

"I went to four different schools. It was awful."

He says that they kept moving because his mum was trying to get them a house with a bathroom inside. Allan is now well-off but he still remembers his life as a child. Perhaps this is why he is such a good writer of books for children.

Allan worked on many of his books with his wife – the **illustrator** Janet Ahlberg. Two of their very famous ones are *Each Peach Pear Plum* and *Peepo!* They got the ideas for lots of their books for young children from watching their own little girl. Sadly, Janet Ahlberg died in 1994.

Janet Ahlberg illustrated many of Allan's books

Allan is a writer who has lots and lots of ideas. He keeps notes of these ideas in an old cigar box. But he doesn't use them all.

He says, "The real skill is in choosing which of your ideas you are going to develop."

Don't you wish you could peep into Allan's box of ideas?

Beatrix Potter

Beatrix Potter is the **author** of *The Story of Miss Moppet* – one of her 30 famous animal stories for children. Beatrix Potter was born in London in 1866 and she died in 1943.

In those days, small children from rich families did not see much of their parents. They spent their time in their part of the house called the nursery. Beatrix was nearly six when her brother Bertram was born, so her first few years in the nursery must have been lonely.

The family spent a lot of time each year on holiday in the Lake District. As well as playing, Beatrix and Bertram would spend time drawing and learning about animals and plants. As soon as he was old enough, Bertram went away to school. Beatrix stayed at home and had lessons from a governess. She was very shy and had no friends.

THE STORY OF
MISS MOPPET

TM

BEATRIX POTTER
THE ORIGINAL AND AUTHORIZED EDITION
New colour reproductions
F. WARNE & CO

Even when she was a young woman, Beatrix still lived in the nursery and carried on with her drawing and painting. She used to paint very lifelike animals but she would often add a scarf to a rabbit or a waistcoat to a frog. As she got older, she used to write letters to the children of friends or governesses. She would send them stories and pictures of her animal friends.

Beatrix Potter thought that she might be able to publish her letters as children's books. She sent her work off to several **publishers** but they did not want it.

Peter Rabbit

This photo of Beatrix Potter was taken in 1892 when she was 26 years old

So, at the age of 35, she herself paid for *The Tale of Peter Rabbit* to be printed. Her family and friends thought it was very good. The publishers Frederick Warne changed their minds. They said they would publish the book if Beatrix would illustrate it in colour.

The Tale of Peter Rabbit was published in October 1902. By Christmas it had sold 28,000 copies. Beatrix quickly wrote and illustrated more stories. She became friends with her **editor** at Frederick Warne and in 1905 they were going to marry. But five weeks after they had got engaged, Norman Warne died.

She bought a farm and went to live in the Lake District. In 1913 she got married to William Heelis. The lonely Beatrix Potter had found someone to share her life.

Beatrix Potter's cottage in the Lake District

Martin Waddell

Martin Waddell

Martin Waddell is the author of *Man Mountain*. He was born in Belfast in 1940 but the family soon went to live by the sea. He used to have a black cat called Tiny and a dog called Joe that he took for walks on the beach. When he was a boy, Martin used to write stories – but he loved playing football more.

Martin wanted to be a professional footballer. As a teenager he went to Fulham Football Club to train as a goalkeeper but his eyesight wasn't good enough.

"I let in too many goals because I couldn't see the ball and then I knew I wasn't going to be a footballer, so I put on my glasses and started writing stories."

While he was living in London, Martin had turned more and more to writing. At last he got a **manuscript** published and the book was made into a film.

This is the town in Ireland where Martin grew up and where he now lives

With the money he made from the film, he went back to Ireland to live – in the town by the sea where he grew up. He still lives in Ireland with his wife Rosaleen and has three sons: Tom, David and Peter.

Like all writers, Martin works hard.

He says, "My **routine** is to go to my room every day, and stay there. I have lots of bits of stories there. I pick one up and work on it. Some of them will never be finished, but they start me working, and then, with luck, I move on to something better."

Martin has written over 160 books and has won many **awards** for his writing. Most of his books are written using his own name but some are written under the name of Catherine Sefton. The books he writes as Catherine Sefton are mostly for older children and teenagers.

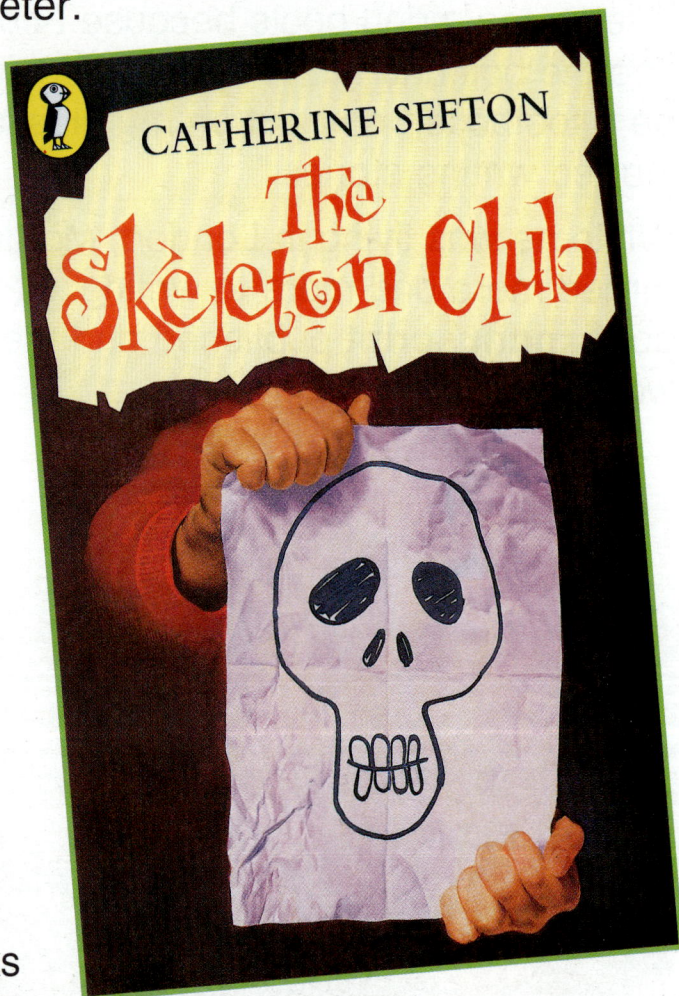

CATHERINE SEFTON

The Skeleton Club

When he is not writing, Martin likes to play a little tennis and walk on the beach and in the mountains. And, of course, he still loves football and writing!

As he says, "Writing is my hobby. I am just lucky enough to get paid for it."

Man Mountain

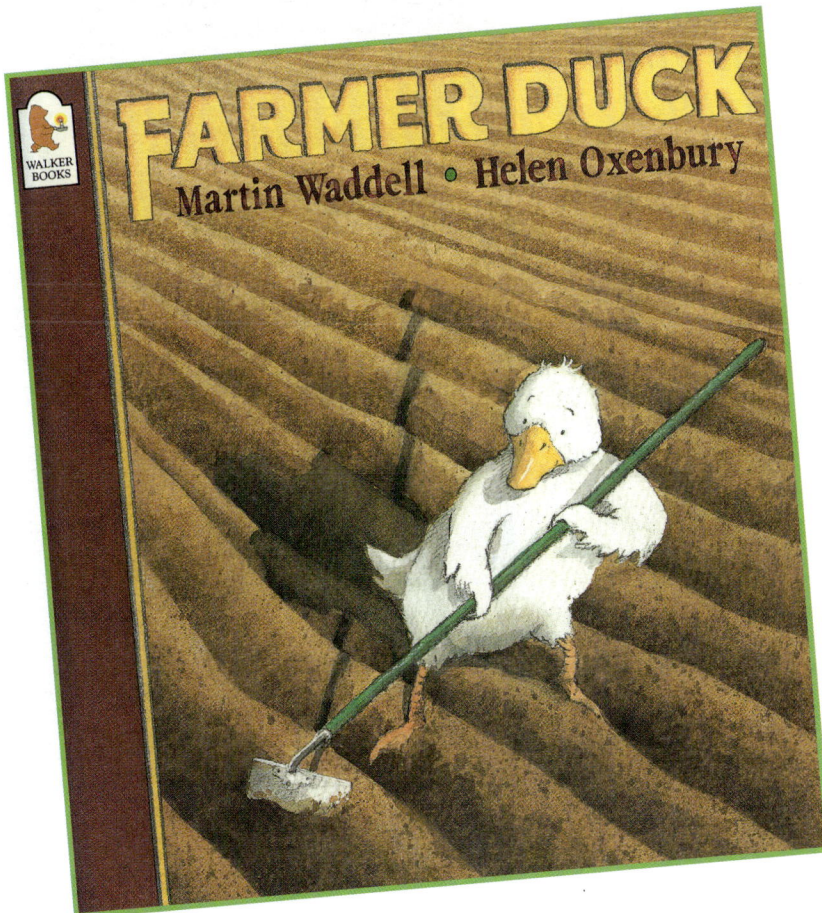

Gene Kemp

When people see Gene Kemp's name on a book cover, they often assume that this writer is a man – but she's not! Gene Kemp is the author of *Matty's Midnight Monster*. It is unusual for Gene to write picture books – she is more famous for her novels for older children.

The **publication date** of Gene Kemp's first book, *The Prime of Tamworth Pig*, was 1972 but she says that she started writing long before that. Her earliest memory of writing was coming home from her first day at school and writing all over her mother's sideboard in chalk. She wrote "Mother see Kitty", and she thought it was lovely. However, her mother was not so pleased!

Gene Kemp

Gene was born in Wigginton, Staffordshire in 1926 but she now lives in Devon. Devon is a beautiful place to live and Gene loves walking on the moors. She also enjoys reading, television, gardening and talking "especially to children".

Like quite a few children's authors, Gene has worked as a teacher. Knowing about children (she is also a grandmother) and about schools is probably one reason why her school stories are so successful.

A **reviewer** said of her books, "No one writes with more insight into the primary school classroom, its pupils or its teachers."

Gene Kemp has won several awards for her writing. Her most widely known book, *The Turbulent Term of Tyke Tiler,* was the first book to receive both the **Carnegie Medal** and the Other Award (1977).

This is the Carnegie Medal Gene was awarded for *The Turbulent Term of Tyke Tiler*

When she was once asked for her advice on how to be a successful writer, Gene said there were three things to remember. Firstly, you have to write something. Secondly, you send it off to a publisher. Thirdly, don't give up when it gets sent back to you – send it off to someone else!

Successful writers usually have little trouble in thinking of ideas for stories and often the smallest thing like something they have seen or heard can spark off an idea.

Gene Kemp says, "Ideas come from all around you and from inside your head. Sometimes they tire me out and I have to say to them firmly, 'Shut up and go away!'."

Catherine Storr

Catherine Storr is the author of *Clever Polly and the Stupid Wolf* and was a writer with a very varied background. She was born in London in 1913 and London is where she made her home.

When she left school, Catherine went to Cambridge University to study English but she decided that she wanted to have a career in medicine instead. She did her training at West London Hospital and worked for 14 years treating people who were mentally ill. Later she worked for a publisher (Penguin Books) as an assistant editor.

Catherine's first book was published in 1940 and she went on to write over 40 books for children – both fiction and non-fiction. Her most famous ones are those about Clever Polly (not forgetting the Wolf!).

Catherine Storr

But Catherine didn't only write for children. She wrote many novels, plays and non-fiction books for adults. She did think, however, that she was better at writing for children.

"I'm a natural storyteller, which is why I'm better and more successful at writing for children, who want a story above everything else, than I am at writing fiction for adults."

Catherine began writing stories when she was seven or eight and said that she couldn't remember a time when she didn't want to write books.

When she was asked what was hard about being a writer she said, "The hardest things about writing are getting down to work and its solitary aspect." (Many authors would agree with her about writing being a lonely job and most writers find that getting started is difficult!)

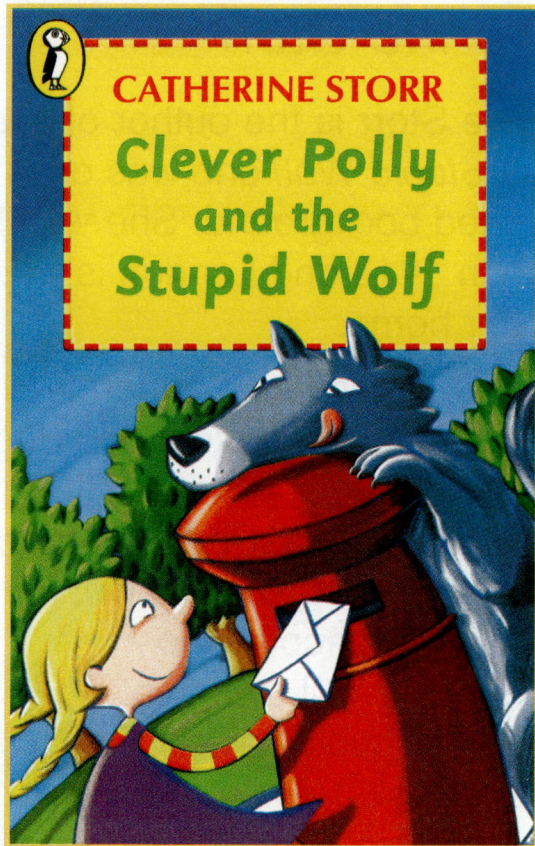

So what did Catherine find exciting about writing?

She once said, "The most exciting thing is being a third of the way through **a work** and knowing that it is going in the right direction ..."

Catherine continued writing until she was an old lady. In the spring of 2000, she was working on dramatising the "Clever Polly and Stupid Wolf" stories.

She died in January 2001, but her books will live on.

Glossary of Words about Writing and Writers

draft	a piece of writing that is not yet finished
full-time writer	someone who earns a living from writing
illustrator	the person who does the pictures in a book
poet	a person who writes poetry
word processor	a kind of computer used for writing and printing

author	the writer of a book, story or play, etc.
award	a prize – usually money
editor	the person who gets the author's manuscript ready for printing as a book
manuscript	what the author has written – typed but not printed
publishers	the people who prepare, print and sell books
routine	the same things done in the same way each time

a work	what the author is writing or has written
Carnegie Medal	a prize awarded each year for an outstanding children's book, written in English and published in the UK
dramatising	making a story into a play
publication date	when a book was first published
reviewer	someone who writes about their opinion of a book